Commit Emotional Suicide

Take Back Your Life

Gregory G. Sansone

ISBN:1507783736
ISBN-13:9781507783733

DEDICATION

This book is dedicated to those who suffer in silence in despair. My life mission is to find each and every one of you.

CONTENTS

ACKNOWLEDGEMENTS

I would like to acknowledge all of those who have been significant in my recovery.

Dr. Alan Tamaren (St. Louis, MO) is the first therapist I ever went to. He is remarkably intelligent, flexible, and insightful. Thank you Alan.

Dr. Steven Phillipson (New York City) is quite possibly the OCD guru as it relates to aggressively challenging the OCD brain. Thanks Steve.

Dr. Reed Simpson (Psychiatrist, St. Louis, MO) is a brilliant man to the 10th power and truly understands effective medication. Thanks Doc. and continued thanks.

Dr. Susan Englund (St. Louis, MO) is brilliant and, all too rare, humble. What a killer combination. She allowed my true recovery to flourish by recognizing that I had a tremendous amount to offer in my personal recovery combined with her brilliance. Thank you Susan. You will never know.

Dr. Reed Wilson I want you to know that your website (anxieties.com) has greatly contributed to my recovery. Thank you. You are very appreciated.

Finally, I would like to thank and acknowledge my wife Mary Ann. She is truly a brilliant, wise, and loving person. She changed my life. Thank you Mary Ann. Without you this book would never have happened. Endless thanks to you.

INTRODUCTION

This books sole purpose is to share what I have learned over 33 years in dealing with OCD. It is also to share with fellow sufferers what I have learned in 9 years of therapy from the Midwest to New York City to the West Coast. I am only sharing the beneficial parts. A lot of time, effort, and expense went into seeking out the best of the best to help myself. I share it all with you.

Five years ago I started the 'Show Me OCD' support groups along with private coaching sessions to help those in distress. This book is another attempt to reach the silent OCD sufferer. I will continue searching for you in any way possible. I remember all too well my painful, scary, clueless, lonely days with OCD. There is more help available now than ever before. The International Obsessive Compulsive Disorder Foundation (IOCDF) is an outstanding resource. They are on the cutting edge of effective treatment. Join the IOCDF. It can change your life.

My purpose in writing this book is only to help. I am in no way suggesting that my way is the only way to recovery. Quite to the contrary, each and every one of us is different and one size does not fit all. I am not a therapist and don't proclaim to be. Please feel 100% comfortable in disagreeing with anything I have written in this book. Sometimes words fall short in conveying one's actual meaning.

It is not words in a book that will get you well. Rather, it is your internal commitment to fight this and to begin experimenting and discovering what works for you. I strongly believe at the heart of recovery is accepting uncertainty and taking risks. Please enjoy my first book and read it with the hope and fire to recover. Your recovery is directly related to how hard you are willing to work. Freedom awaits. Go for it!

CHAPTER ONE

MY OCD

I have had OCD since I was 18 years old. It literally started all of a sudden, out of nowhere. I'm now 51 years old and it wasn't until I was 44 that I discovered the treatment and path that would radically change my life. Through a lot of research and searching, I came in contact with a therapist out of New York City, Dr. Stephen Phillipson. I had found the help I needed. I went from a 40 percent improvement to about 70 in only 2 months, and in 4 months I was at or above 80%. Dr. Stephen Phillipson is a wonderful OCD specialist. I love his aggressive, attack approach and his commitment to Exposure Response Prevention.

In my experience (both personal and with group members) it was and is all too rare to come across a therapist who was truly effective in precipitating real recovery from OCD, though they do exist. I soon began discovering and developing subtle tips and nuances on my own which were profoundly instrumental in taking back the life that was snatched from my grasp some 30 years ago. It is these nuances and tips I want to share with all OCD sufferers. This book is dedicated and written to you and the courage that is within you to commit to taking back what was stolen from you. It can be done and I am committed to you knowing and experiencing the success in overcoming OCD as I have and continue to.

OCD is obsessive compulsive disorder. There are obsessions and there are compulsions. An obsession is an unwanted, intrusive, repetitive thought, image, or urge. This intrusion causes us great anxiety in which we try to do something to make the anxiety go away. The thing that we do to try to make the anxiety go away is called a compulsion. A compulsion is an action or repetitive ritual that is designed to remove anxiety immediately in the moment. Compulsions can be physical as well as mental in nature. The problem with compulsions is that they cause OCD to get stronger because we are highlighting it by responding to it in such an anxious, urgent manner. We are telling our brains that this obsession is very relevant and is very important by the simple fact that we are doing the compulsion. So our brains will bring it back to us again. Whatever is important to us our brains will remind us of, so every time we do a compulsion, a ritual, we tap 3, avoid stepping on a crack, every time we do that, so as to avoid, you know, breaking our mother's back or avoid injury coming to our family by tapping for example, we are feeding OCD. We are reinforcing the anxiety and the powerful urge to get rid of it right now. That's a very harmful, unhealthy thing to do and it continues to make the groove, the neural pathway, in our brain more engrained. As the groove becomes deeper and deeper from reinforcement it becomes harder and harder to break the habit. The problem with compulsing is that in the short run it does work, so we get a reward by doing it. At the risk of over simplifying, it's like a drug addict. The problem with drugs is that on some level they work. The drug addict feels relief, or high or euphoric or whatever the emotional state is that the drug gives them, so then it becomes more important and you want it more. The problem with it, as we all know, is the addiction, after effects, the detox, the coming down, and the overall loss of control of our lives as happens with both drugs and OCD. The quick fix in the moment is not the answer. That is one of the most important points in this book...the quick fix in the moment to make ourselves feel better is not the answer.

My Obsessions

I've had numerous obsessions over the years. I've had magical thinking, sensorimotor obsessions, fear of going crazy, scrupulosity... moral and religious, and social anxiety. The fear of going crazy was a particularly very, very powerful theme for me and it manifested itself in very intense obsessions. The obsession, the first that ever came to me was, "What if something fell out of the sky and hit me?" I think the reason it came to me was because of the pressing question, "How can I make sure I will never go crazy?" That fear developed when the OCD hit me, or 'popped' as Stephen Phillipson calls it. This fear was preceded by an experience with a depth of anxiety, depression, emptiness, and sheer terror that I had never felt before. It made me feel like I was going to go crazy. In response to that frightening experience, I set out on a mission to prove to myself that I wasn't going to go crazy EVER and to MAKE SURE that would NEVER happen. "How could I prove to myself that I wouldn't ever go crazy?" I obsessed about that idea and created compulsions that I thought were improving my situation and lessening my anxiety. In actuality, I was making it worse and looking for trouble. I was looking for problems and of course I discovered that, yes, I 'could' go crazy. Anyone can convince themselves that they could go crazy if they play the 'what if' game.... what if? "What if... what if something fell out of the sky and hit me? Living everyday knowing that that possibility exists would put me in a state of fear and constant panic which would cause me to go crazy, wouldn't it?" This was my line of thinking. It felt irresponsible not to be concerned about something that was possible. So I felt compelled to figure it out. I thought I had to be missing something, otherwise, "wouldn't all responsible, adult people be as stuck and concerned about this as I was?" This was how my thinking went. I had never thought this way until then.

Another obsession, along the same vein, was regarding the after-life. I was raised to believe that when we die we either go to heaven, hell, or purgatory. We were taught that most likely we were going to purgatory for a period of time first so naturally I started imagining what purgatory would be like. "What if it was like scratching your nails on a chalk board feeling? What if it was that?" The idea of running my nails down a chalk board... I couldn't imagine how horrific that would be, and then, because I was on this search to find a guarantee that I wouldn't go crazy, my next thought was, "Well what if... what if nails going down a chalk board is actually the experience of what hell is... which is forever, not just temporary like purgatory. How do I know that I won't go to hell?" Wow! I had found more evidence that I COULD go crazy because of certain possibilities that I couldn't reason away. There was always "what if!" "If I could find a way to not dwell on this possibility, I might not go crazy now." But I still couldn't reason away the thought that when I died I could, maybe and forever, go to hell (nails scratching down a chalk board feeling for all eternity.) I would go crazy there and that would definitely be forever with no escape! Complete panic and anxiety set in which, if I was honest with myself, I could not reason away. This was my line of thinking and reasoning. I was trying to be as honest with myself as possible in searching for my "guarantee" that I would never go crazy. I couldn't tolerate having the thought that it was possible...no matter how small that possibility was that I 'could' go crazy. "Well, if you do this and do this and do this, then you won't got to hell they say, but how in the hell do they know for sure?! What if they are wrong? What if?! What if I'm supposed to be doing this or not supposed to be doing that and I don't know which way is right because God never told me?" I couldn't find any hard evidence of it... what if? And the logical answer, in this sick sense of reasoning, was that it is possible and I could and maybe would go to hell. I would have to endure fingernails scratching down a chalkboard for all of eternity... over and over and over and over and over again. This fear of going crazy permeated throughout all of my different obsessions.

An obsession I had, and still can have at times, was what they call sensorimotor obsessions. I didn't learn what that word was until later in my recovery process. It sure felt good to know there was a name for it. Sensorimotor obsessions have to do with any obsession that is associated with the normal, involuntary functions of the body such as: blinking, swallowing, how to think, how to actually talk and walk (things we just do naturally that we don't think about,) sweating, feeling, rhythm and cadence, the sound of my voice, digestion, and definitely sleeping and dreaming during sleep. This was a powerful, powerful fearful category for me and was right in line with my 'go to' freak-out theme of "How can I be sure I will never go crazy?" And I still think that's how this one came about. I was trying to prove to myself that I could never go crazy by trying to think of the worst, most unimaginable things possible in order to see if I could handle them and how. I created them in my mind and it was like, "What if I forgot how to sleep?" Wow... never thought about that one before. Just like we never think about swallowing or digesting our food... our bodies just do it. But now I had to control all of these functions so I could prove to myself I WOULD NEVER go crazy as a result of not being able to do these things or go crazy as a result that now that this has been brought to my attention I won't ever be able to blink, sleep, or swallow naturally because I won't be able to stop thinking about it (that one can still get me today.) I needed to be in control of this! As you can imagine, my OCD started to spiral out of control. "So how do I sleep?" Okay. So I started to try and make myself sleep to prove that I was in control of that function, to prove that I would never not sleep and go crazy. Wow. As you know, it doesn't work that way. Forcing ourselves to try to go to sleep usually ends up with the opposite result. So then I started to panic, "Oh my God I can't sleep!" "I'm gonna go crazy"... "What if I never sleep again??!!" I had read that the lack of sleep could actually make you go crazy or die or cause some other horrible thing to happen. "How can I get a grip on this?" And I thought, "Oh my God, I can't!!!!" I'm going to be in a horrible state of fear, anxiety, fatigue, and embarrassment because people will notice how tired I look." That is when my social anxiety began. "This will be a miserable, horrible life and I could go crazy from it and be in perpetual agony for all eternity with no escape" - very, very cheerful thoughts.

My sensorimotor obsessions manifested themselves in many other different ways as well... the sound of my voice, thinking, and all the other things that I mentioned... blinking, swallowing, how often am I supposed to blink? And the looking at people one! "How do I properly look at someone when they say you should look people in their eyes... ok... let's get that down pat. How do I do that? How DO I look at someone and what is the RIGHT way to look at them? And it was like well, as soon as I ask the question I got a problem because there is no hard and fast answer to an obsessive, ANXIOUS, urgent question like that. Well, okay, you look at them in the eyes. Okay, but they got two eyes... okay well I read a book once that said you look at one eye... okay... I look at one eye. Okay, that frees it up... but wait a minute, I have two eyes. How are two eyes supposed to look at one thing? Do I have one eye looking at one thing and one eye looking at another? One eye looking at an eye and one looking...????" How do you do that? How do ya?!?! As you can imagine, the feeling that I was going to lose my mind was very prevalent. This "how do you look at someone" obsession was powerful. To this day that obsession still comes back to bother me. "How do I look at someone??" And every time I think about it, I have a tendency to get messed up. I have found the solution though... I will get into that later.

By becoming so obsessed with my eyes and how they look and looked I noticed one eye was a little tighter than the other. That's when I decided, "Okay, wait a minute, the way to look at somebody the right way is to have both eyes really relaxed so I can have kind of a comfortable gaze. That's the way to do it. Okay great! So, just get both of my eyes relaxed"... of course the exact opposite starts to happen. I notice a little tension in one eye, and the thought comes in, "What if my eye gets more tense and I can't relax and look at someone the right way and then they think I'm crazy??!! What if my eye does the opposite of relax and it gets tighter and tighter and tighter?! I'll look like an insane person! They will lock me up forever"... okay, not good. "Also what if I am, although this has more to do with my moral and religious scrupulosity, possessed by the devil and this tightening of the eye is evidence of that and people run from me in terror because they think I have the devil in me... I look like a monster because my eye is so tight???!!!!" Wow!

Then there is my social anxiety obsession about sweaty palms. I go to shake hands with somebody and I notice that my palms are sweaty and I think, "Oh that's embarrassing, wipe them off, and then it's like well wait a minute, "what if?"... there we go again. What if that never stopped? What if the sweating continued? What if I shook somebody's hand and mine was soaking wet and they looked at me in disgust and disrepute, and they said to me, "What is wrong with you, your hands are SOAKING WET!!!!!!?" How embarrassing and humiliating!! It was always very important to me to come off strong, together, and controlled. That attitude fed my anxiety and made my palms start to sweat in public. The more I tried to 'not' make it happen, the more it would happen. You talk about a mind screw!

As far as 'humor and the sound of my voice' obsession goes, when people say to me, "Oh, you have a wonderful voice, you really have a great speaking voice," I think, "well okay, how do I make sure I do that all of the time? How can I make my voice always sound good? Well dummy, you don't... you leave it alone. The problem is I can't leave it alone because now I'm focused on it. If I could and did leave this fear alone, my nice voice might sound bad because I can't guarantee that it wouldn't change on its own and I would get embarrassed. How can I control it and make sure I will always have a great voice so I will always be able to make a good living, always be liked by people, liked enough to always have people around me, to support me, and be my friends... so I won't be alone and isolated and hopeless and helpless for all eternity!!" This was how my thinking went. The more I tried to make my voice relaxed, the more tense my throat felt and the odder and less pleasing I felt it sounded to others. I was quite effective doing phone sales. I'd close a deal and I was convinced it was because of the way I spoke to people... the way I came across to people. So, of course, I asked myself, "How do I control that so I never lose the ability to make my voice sound good to others... so I never go broke and my family never has to starve and die?"... wonderful line of thinking… all OCD.

I also, amidst the other obsessions, began experiencing scrupulosity... moral and religious. This scrupulosity basically occurred when I was trying to follow Catholic doctrine to the law. My obsession was "what is a sin?"

"How do I know if it is a sin or not. When I pass a guy on the road and I was mad, I didn't say anything but I had angry thoughts... how do I know that wasn't a sin and bad, or more?" "What if I did something wrong, you know, I lied and God punished me? He may not let me sleep at night. Or, you know, what if I was not completely honest with somebody when I spoke with them or complimented them... didn't say everything... the whole truth? Or what if I did something that I thought MIGHT be wrong... what if God didn't bless me? And what if I wasn't in God's good graces? Then I wouldn't know how to look at someone or I wouldn't have relaxed eyes. And so it is this line of thinking and scrupulosity that persists even today, albeit much less. I still question myself in business. For example, if I'm thinking how to win or succeed at something, I'll think, "Well now wait a minute, is that fair? Maybe that guy hasn't thought of this." Then I think, "Well wait a minute, common sense tells me that's just competition. I know if I do a better job or I out-think the other person then I will succeed. But maybe that's wrong. Maybe that's kind of sneaky, deceitful.... maybe I won't sleep tonight or I won't know how to look at someone or I won't have relaxed eyes." You get the picture... all of that type of thinking… OCD garbage!

My compulsion was "a figuring out." Whenever any of my obsessions would come to my mind, I would have to figure it out... like having to figure out if it really is true that God can make my eye tight because I wasn't completely honest about something? To have to figure it out if my punishment would be having a tight eye instead of a relaxed eye, which would cause me to not be able to look at somebody with comfort and peace. I would have to figure that out, reason that away, so I would no longer believe that... clearly a compulsion... the "figuring out" compulsion. It's what I would do to relieve my anxiety in the moment as a result of the thought... the thought that was an obsession that said, "God may cause THIS if I don't clean this up because I wasn't totally honest." The obsession of 'what if my hands sweat when I have to shake hands,' compelled me to figure out how to make my hands not sweat when I go out in public. And I was compelled to figure out how to reason away the eternal fingernail chalkboard obsession. I needed to figure out how to feel just right. I needed to make sure I felt just right... be at my absolute best so people will think highly of me. I needed to not be vulnerable. I needed to be totally confident and totally with it and strong. I needed to figure out how to make both my eyes relaxed... try to keep my hands and feet dry and to not perspire at all. It's just basically the feeling of having it all together first and then going out into the world... figuring it all out, getting it all together and then going out and living in the real world. I soon learned that the counter to that is so much more productive... going unready. We will get more into that in later chapters. It's very powerful to go unready.

So again, my compulsion was to figure stuff out that was in my head... to spend hours on it, thinking on it... which only made it get worse and worse. Every time I came up with something that felt good like, "Okay I will believe 'that' more than 'this,' so I'm not afraid," then I'd have the thought, "Yah, but 'what if this?' or 'what if that?'" Oh my God it was exhausting, literally exhausting and depressing and it made my self-esteem and my self-confidence plummet. Every time I would give in and do the compulsion, it would make my OCD worse because I was reinforcing the relevance of the obsession. I was reinforcing how important it was to me which signaled to my brain, "This must be important because he's responding this way, so next time this happens I will respond even more emphatically." I am telling my brain how important it is by how I respond to it when it is there. So every time it showed up, I would have a five-alarm fire that said, "Hey, hey, hey, things are bad! You better attend to this! You better because you did last time, it's important!!" The best way to handle it is to not respond to it.... don't respond...no compulsion.

CHAPTER TWO

EXPOSURE RESPONSE PREVENTION

Exposures, Exposure Response Prevention, ERP - whatever you want to call it - is the gold standard treatment for OCD. A lot of people don't like to do it because it's difficult work. I am always urging people to remember that having OCD every day is difficult work as well. It is tough having OCD and it's tough getting rid of OCD. The difference is when you do the exposures and get rid of it, you are free. If you refuse to work on it... you just keep enduring, day after day... after day in continuous imprisonment sacrificing the only life you have.

So the way exposure therapy works is like this, you take the obsession - the fear that bothers you, that freaks you out, whatever it is - and purposely brings it to your awareness. Your goal is to make yourself anxious and to prove to your brain that the obsession is irrelevant. We show our mind that OCD is irrelevant to us by not running from our fear... we are showing our mind that this fear is irrelevant. We do this by allowing ourselves to feel anxious without resistance (not as hard as you may think.) The results will make you a believer, let alone, make you feel powerful and joyful. We also show our mind that this concern, this obsession we are having, is unimportant to us by not changing our choices or plans... even though it scares us. We are showing our mind that, yes not only are we not running from this scary stuff, but we are calling it out. "Come on, come make me anxious." Furthermore, we show the irrelevance by getting on with our lives as soon as the exposure is over - regardless of how off, tight-eyed, or lousy we may feel. This all interrupts the OCD cycle. It shows our mind that this obsession doesn't have any power over us. Ultimately, by doing this repeatedly, it results in our mind not delivering the obsession to us. Freedom.... that is our goal. It's very difficult to wrap one's mind around this idea because the nature of anxiety - with our natural "fight or flight" response - is that when we are anxious, that is a signal to us that something is wrong and we need to fix it. We have to override that and the way to do that is through repetition... practicing repeatedly, over and over and over again... doing the exposures over and over again. This has to be #1 in your life. It can be done and it is the access to being OCD free.

So we expose ourselves to the feared stimulus. We do not try to make ourselves 'not' anxious. Actually, we have created a new relationship with anxiety. We view anxiety as good; anxiety is a good thing. "When we are willingly allowing ourselves to be anxious, we are winning." (Dr. Reed Wilson). We are winning because we are allowing the anxiety to be there, and we are allowing it by preventing the response we normally have when we are trying to make it go away, and we are adding to it, "I want this anxiety." This is the response prevention part... not doing the compulsion... not doing the thing that we always do to make ourselves feel better when the scary thought or urge comes to us. We are no longer doing that. We are breaking the pattern. The brain only brings us stuff with urgency that it thinks is important and relevant to us. We show it that it is important or not by our response to it. By not responding to it in a fearful manner we are actually beginning to kill off OCD. Our brain will eventually stop sending the obsession... awesome stuff!!!

There are different ways to do exposures and I have tried most of them. One formal structured exposure that has worked really well for me is with the use of a tape recorder. You speak your fear into the recorder and listen to it over and over and over again. Put it on loop so there is about a ten second pause between the repeating message. You feel the anxiety and keep listening to it anyway. When your anxiety comes down to at least half of what it was at its highest point you can turn the recorder off. This can take anywhere from thirty minutes to 2 hours, depending on how intense the obsession is for you.

Another example of a formal structured exposure is to use index cards. Write your obsession on the card... the thought that comes to your mind... that freaks you out. Read it to yourself with meaning; presence yourself to it.

Make it real. Look away for ten or fifteen seconds and let the anxiety settle in. Maybe mark it on a card on scale of 1 to 10 of how high it goes (Phillipson). Do that. Do that every day with any fear or obsession that you have that disrupts your life. Then do nothing to make the anxiety go away. So those are a couple examples of structured exposures.... remarkably powerful.

I actually exposed myself to my fear of going to hell until it no longer scared me - never thought that was possible - but it was. When you reach boredom during your exposures you know that you are over that particular fear. Whether you think your concern is real, valid, or not, don't try to figure it out, just do the exposure to remove the fear that it causes. See what happens... see where it takes you first. Don't figure it out first for fear that it could be valid and not OCD... you are fighting OCD, so treat it as such. Boredom is the goal. The only way to reach this boredom is to make anxiety the goal. It's contrary to the way we have dealt with OCD in the past but it absolutely works. You want to make yourself as anxious as often as possible and when you do that over and over and over again through your exposures, boredom will arrive. You have to seek out anxiety over and over again until you have reached the point where you simply cannot feel anxious anymore. This is when boredom arrives. Moving from anxiety into boredom is an amazingly beautiful experience. You will soon determine how much you dislike boredom... but beats the hell out of fear!!

There are also what are called 'in the moment' exposures. For example, something happens that makes you anxious while you are going about your day. When this happens, you simply, in the moment, remember that this is good. This is that moment, that opportunity, to allow the anxiety to be there.... embrace it. Ask it to stay as long as it can. Expose to the fear first then you can think about it or talk about it if you still want to once you are not afraid of it. Don't try to escape that feeling. Hold onto it, hang out in in, and go about your day with that unpleasant feeling until it leaves on its own. Ask yourself this simple question, "Can you really not stand this a second longer?" Continue to hold. Give it no mental resistance. This is what kills OCD. This is the treatment for OCD. I am standing, living proof that it works.

Absolutely awesome! Try it and find out. Don't ask questions. Try it for yourself and see! Talking about it is of very little benefit. It's in the doing. There are no rules. There's no need for perfection. Do it in your own style. You are the architect of your exposure. Experiment with it.

The goal is to allow yourself to be anxious when it comes to you... to allow it to stay for as long as it does. The treatment is to be as anxious as possible as often as possible. Do not resist it or try to feel better in that moment. Having the presence of mind to remind yourself of that idea comes through the repetition of going over your cards, memos, notes, and listening to your recordings.... all to help you remember that anxiety is your friend. You may say that being anxious as often as possible doesn't work because you have been anxious for years with this X!!?XG OCD! True. You have been anxious for many years struggling with your OCD, but I can guarantee that you were resisting the anxiety and wishing it would leave... doing everything you knew possible to make it go away. The treatment is both parts: being anxious and not trying to make the anxiety go away.

When it leaves on its own, while having the invitation from you to stay, major progress is being made in your recovery. On the other hand, when you chase it out the door, you have guaranteed its return. Which is what we do when we are caught in the OCD cycle of obsessions and compulsions. That's just how the mind and OCD work... very powerful.

We want to approach our exposures audaciously and boldly as opposed to fearfully and frailly... with a victimized approach. We want to bring on the fear... bring on the anxiety. We want to go after resilience. We don't want to go after relief during the exposure. That's not the goal that we look for while we are doing exposures. Resilience to endure the fear for as long as possible, is what we are after. We are not seeking relief. Don't look for that with OCD... period. Relief will find you... after you do your work. Go for the resilience. How long can you take it? Be bold. Be radical. The faster your anxiety gets to its highest point... the quicker you get to feeling your worst, the quicker it will subside. You have to reach that high point and when you do, for some - for the first time ever, you will experience true freedom. You can only experience it... not talk about it. You want to burn out the anxiety through exposures. You want to burn it out... you want to let it flood you until there's no more anxiety left in you to feel. That's how you kill it. That is how you kill that particular fear, that particular obsession.

An important distinction I learned is that when you are doing your exposure, you're not trying to convince yourself that your fear will not come true... NO. You are trying to NO LONGER FEAR the thing HAPPENING which you now fear... that's all... that's it. All you are trying to do with exposures is remove the fear. You're not trying to convince yourself that you're not going to hell. You're not trying to convince yourself that you won't die from cancer because you drove past a hospital that has a cancer wing. That is not exposure. Exposure is for the purpose of letting this fear beat your ass. You're going to see how long you can take it and when you do that... when it gets to its worst point, tie a knot and hang on. You are right there at freedom's door. It will drop. The anxiety will begin to drop. Try it. You want to go for the removal of the fear and that is done by scaring ourselves fearless. Get rid of the fear of the topic or issue first.

Then if you want to have a philosophical discussion about it later, about that particular issue, that's fine, but don't talk about it or think about it when you are afraid of it... when it's an obsession that gets you caught in the OCD trap. The quicker you bring it on, the quicker it will burn itself out. You remove the fear that it causes first. That's what exposures are for.

If you are using cards for exposures, you want to write down exactly the way your mind delivers the fear to you. However your mind says it, you want to duplicate that as closely as possible... write that down on your card or speak it into your recorder so it scares the shit out of you. You want to make it as real as possible and as real a fear as possible. This isn't just some exercise that isn't real. This is real! These exposures are real... real and real scary. The beautiful thing about it is you are very close to freedom when you are your most scared. Then you will see it drop. Just hang on. I read somewhere that just when you think you are going to pass out... you are choking and you can't take it any longer, if you hold on all of a sudden you hit freedom and it stops. That is figurative language of course, but the point being is if you are committed to that degree, you WILL BREAK FREE. The point I am trying to make is that when you feel like quitting, don't. You are close, centimeters from freedom of your anxiety dropping and you making a break-through... a new awareness... a new FREEDOM... extremely important!

I'm going to walk you through one of my exposures to give you an example. This was the first time I really experienced the true benefits of exposure and how it works. I broke through the anxiety and I hit that place of freedom. A place that, right before that, was filled with incredible fear, but I hung because I was doing and believing in the treatment. You have to have faith in the treatment. Don't question it, try it. We love to question it because it helps us avoid trying it... it keeps us in a 'safe place'... miserably safe, and depressed. Ok, so I used to fear that God could do bad things to me. He could keep me up at night. He could cause my eye to get tight. He could cause one eyebrow to rise up. He could strike me dead. He could cause me to go blind. He could make me stop breathing on the spot. God could do anything. He could have something drop on me from the sky. "God

could do anything to me!" That was my thought...
incredibly, remarkably frightening. So, in my OCD days I
would counter that thought by saying, "God is not like
that. He made nature. It's beautiful. He loves us. He
doesn't want to do that. He's not some evil, sick guy," but
OCD would say, "Yah, but how do you know? Animals
fight animals. Animals eat animals. Maybe God has a
mean side too. He created that you know. He could have
made them all vegetarians... maybe God is crazy." And
then I would get the feeling that, "Holy cow, God could
do anything to us!" I finally realized what a deep fear that
was for me so I wrote it down on a card: "God could do
anything to me" and I sat down and I read it. I sat there
for ten or fifteen seconds. I let myself get as scared as I
could. Once it kind of settled in and I felt it, I would read
it again with meaning and presence... and I kept doing it.
It was scaring the hell out of me. I remember sitting in
my chair, looking up at the corner of the room, having
this remarkable fear and saying to myself, "You know
what, I'm gonna see about this. I'm gonna see about
scaring myself fearless... and I'm going to let it happen.
Good. Scare the hell out of me." I was so scared that I
was almost shaking. My whole body was experiencing the

fear and all I can say (my words pale in comparison to the reality of it) is that when the fear broke, MY WORLD CHANGED. The remarkable fear had broken. "I" didn't break it... it just broke. All I did was try to have the resilience to take it... let it build. When I did that, it broke - it stopped scaring me. The best way I can explain it - the best illustration - is that it felt like A BRAND NEW WORLD FOR ME. One that I had NEVER known before and I didn't think was possible. Like "Oh my God, this doesn't scare me! This is what I have ALWAYS wanted! This is a remarkable new freedom THAT I HAVE NEVER KNOWN!" I never could know it by thinking about it, by asking questions about it. I had to do it to know it, as do you. That's what's so exciting about doing exposure work and getting rid of our obsessions... our fears. It is so powerful! The degree of freedom I experienced was just invigorating... invigorating.!

Do exposures... go to support groups... and continue to do exposures! Get on my website. Interact with me. Get on my mailing list. Stay on it. Make exposures number one in your life! Make it number one over your family, number one over your friends, over your business. I'm not saying you neglect the others, but the way to get over OCD is to make it the number one priority in your life. And the way to do that is through daily and consistent Exposure Response Prevention where you are committed to scaring yourself fearless... the place where there is no more fear left to scare you. Sometimes my fears were so deep I had to do two hours of exposures a day. I would have to walk and move around to stay awake, alert, and present. You want to try and stay alert... whatever you have to do to make yourself present. Keep reminding yourself that when it breaks, it really breaks. Sometimes it takes two or three days, usually a couple of sessions. Studies suggest that 5 to 7 hours of exposure will break a compulsion. Some are longer, some not. Whatever, the point is that exposures truly work... your anxiety will drop. Pour it on. There has been nothing more important in my recovery than exposures done daily - in the moment ones and structured ones with a courageous, bold, and audacious attitude. Go on spike hunts... hunt for things that scare the shit out of you. Write it down and say, "Thank you. There's my next exposure. There's my next path to freedom." Be on a mission to rid yourself of all your mental fears.

CHAPTER THREE

CRITICAL INSIGHTS

We never want to argue with OCD. The obsession; the thing that causes us to be afraid is the poison. The poison neutralizer is ambiguity - not debating or fighting the obsession. This basically means that the obsession, the thought, comes to you and says, "Hey, how do you know you won't die of cancer because you drove by the hospital?" That thought is the poison. You have no control or anything to say as to whether that thought will come to you or not. You don't need to. The next thing that happens is what is most important and something you do have control over. You simply don't answer it or say 'who knows.' Don't debate it, and accept the anxiety that follows. Your goal is to not answer the obsession (question.) Pay attention to your response to the question more than the question itself that comes to your mind. Pay attention to whether you start trying to reason away the concern... wrong thing to do. Pay attention as to whether you allow the question or concern to just hang out there with no response from you... just hang out there in that feeling... right thing to do. Pay attention to whether you feel anxious or not and whether or not you allow the anxiety or uncomfortable feeling to just be there, in your head, or in your body if it wants to. Offer no resistance to this annoying, scary, intrusive thought - then get back into REALITY in the present moment, as opposed to getting involved with some question about what may or may not happen in the future.

We can get back into the present moment by paying attention to what we are doing in that actual moment. If you are driving, continue to drive. If you are listening to the radio, continue to listen to the radio. Put your attention there. At first this may be very hard to do. It will get easier and more natural to do with time and work. This is the practice. This is the work that takes us out of OCD's grip and into the freedom to live our life. The solution is to do productive behavior anyway while feeling anxious. If you do this long enough, the thought (obsession) will stop bothering you. You never want to get in the ring with OCD and start playing the ping-pong match in your head - to try reasoning your way out. That's one thing you don't want to do. This tip can be summed up by saying, "Don't answer the question. Instead, live with any ensuing anxiety until it leaves on its own... which it will if you accept it, make room for it, and allow it stay for as long as it wishes. STAY OUT OF IT. NO DEBATING IT. KEEP YOUR ATTENTION AND ENERGIES OUT OF IT AND GO ON WITH YOUR DAY WHILE FEELING ANXIOUS. YOU WON'T BE DISAPPOINTED WITH THE RESULTS."

Another tip is to always keep in mind what your ultimate goal is. What is your ultimate goal? Why are you doing this? Why are you trying to make yourself anxious? The answer of course is because you want to be free of OCD. You want to be free of this problem. You are tired of being OCD's slave. And that is why you are purposely trying to make yourself anxious…very important to keep that in mind because otherwise you won't do it. You will just go for the immediate relief right now. You'll just go for the hot fudge sundae now instead of not eating it because you want to be and feel healthier later. Keep the ultimate goal in mind, that you want freedom from this. You want to be the director of your life...not OCD. You want your only life back!

Another insight I discovered in dealing with OCD is that when you are having an obsessive thought or fear, act as if it was your friend that was having this and what advice would you give him or her? Then you go follow that same advice. That will give you the objectivity, the space, possibly to be able to look at it from a healthier place. So act like your problem was your friends, what would you say if your friend said to you: "Hey, I saw a 17 on this car today and that could mean God wants me to be catholic and that if I don't change and do that then I may not sleep tonight and go to hell because I may be out of God's Grace." What would your advice be if a friend said that to you? Basically my advice would be to respond by saying that that's the nuttiest X!!?#g thing I have ever heard and you can't live like that. I would then go on to say that you have to make the choice and take the stance to live a healthy, rational, sane life and that's not sane to live according to that shit. So, act as if it was your friend and you were giving him advice and then go and follow that advice for yourself...sometimes that really helps me, but don't make this a compulsion. If it becomes one, drop it.

Another tip is that instead of going after certainty, certainty seeking, instead of doing that go after discovery... just see what happens. Make your mission and your goal to see what happens as it happens only, not to be certain or to make yourself feel good. Discover, to discover what is actually so in that moment and then the OCD or the fear will say: " what if this happens and you really don't sleep? What happens if you are around a bunch of people and your hands are sweating and they are sweating so bad that they are soaking wet?" The response is: no response at all or "We'll see" or "Oh" and then get busy doing something. That is what cuts the OCD cycle... the not figuring it out. Not going in ready. Go in unready and simply have a goal, which is that of discovery, living life NOW and ONLY NOW, going in, and WE WILL SEE. "I am not living life before life happens! I am living it as it happens and I am not preparing. Well, do you think you will be able to handle it? I don't know, we'll see. Well what will you do if you can't handle it? We'll see." Then you cut it and at some point your answer is constantly "we'll see, I don't know if I can handle it but I'm going in anyway," or no response at all, and that feels crazy and it is exactly what is needed in overcoming OCD. It is exactly the opposite of what we are accustomed to doing in trying to make ourselves feel protected, comfortable, and certain as OCD continues to run and destroy our lives. Most importantly, remember what your #1 commitment in your life is. It is to get over OCD at ANY cost, including not sleeping, sweaty palms, possible humiliation, and whatever other possibilities the OCD part of your brain can come up with. This is war. Approach it as war and you will overcome OCD… your #1 priority. Achieve this first and THEN go from their not before (such as right now.) Be 100% committed to overcoming OCD. Live in that given moment only… every time. You will love it!!

Another tip or insight is the use of commands. Giving ourselves commands so that when we are in those obsessional moments and our brain freezes up and we don't think as good because our anxiety is so high... that in those moments we can access commands that we have embedded in our brain or we can pull out our index cards to remind us. The commands can be anything that resonates with you to help you get on the path of healthiness... to risk, to do exposures, to do good productive behavior - not living in your head with thinking but doing and letting the chips fall where they may. Don't try to figure it out or plan for it. That's quicksand. My commands are very simple and to the point, one or two words: "move," "go," "do," "discover," "be uncertain," "hold," "do not compulse," "we will see," "get out," "be a good soldier"... what does that mean?...

"BE A GOOD SOLDIER?" I discovered the idea of being a 'good soldier' at one of IOCDF's annual conferences. A speaker on one of the panels was attesting to his experience with OCD and his recovery. He was a marine. He said he knew that if he stopped doing the compulsions, responding to the fear in the unhealthy way that was attempting to make him feel good in the moment... if he stopped taking that drug, he knew that the OCD would eventually STOP and he would be FREE. So he finally looked at his OCD like it was the enemy and that this enemy was trying to destroy his family, which it was. He refused to ever do another compulsion. He was powerfully motivated to STOP. That was how he empowered himself and that is what eventually took him out of OCD hell. And the longer he did it, refusing to do compulsions, the freer he became and the less it bothered him. So I got to thinking, "Why was this guy able to implement this strategy so well?" It is so difficult to just simply not do a compulsion when you feel like you are dying. I finally realized it was because he is a soldier, literally. He was used to taking orders, directives, and following through with them, period. So he gave himself an order as if he was in the line of duty (and he was, as we must be to get better.) His superior (himself) would command: "GO FORWARD, MOVE, GET OUT" "DO EXPOSURES." That's why and how he stopped doing his compulsions. He was conditioned to be a soldier, as we are all called to be in recovery. He was conditioned to not worry about the mood he was in when a command or directive was given. If he was gonna follow the COMMAND, his mood had to have nothing to do with it. He put himself in that mindset. So I started using that metaphor, 'be a good soldier, be a good soldier.' Use your commands in that moment of obsession and no matter how you feel, follow them. Be a good soldier. You don't have the luxury of saying, "Lieutenant, I'm really not in the mood today to go into battle. I'm really feeling scared, I'm really feeling confused, and I'm really not..." it doesn't matter what you are feeling, you go. And that's the attitude we need in overcoming OCD, it is that of a soldier.

The other metaphor I use for myself is that of a robot... to act like a robot as much as possible in those really tough moments. I say to myself: "Robo-Boy, Robot-Boy. Plug yourself into the commands that will take you out of the loop and onto your feet... living and discovering, rather than spinning your wheels seeking after certainty by "figuring out" in your head ahead of time (the OCD trap.)" Live, do, and move as a robot when you are your most challenged and your OCD or depression has you so down. You plug a robot in with information and it goes automatically. Get on automatic mode - very mechanical but do it (this is the moment of choice.) You don't have to feel it. You don't have to feel good about it. You don't have to believe in it. You don't have to find relief from it. You don't have to have anything. All you gotta do is do it. It doesn't matter how shitty you do it, how good you do it, how effective it feels or how effective it doesn't feel. You must just do it because that is where the healing is. That's the treatment. Be a good soldier Robo-Boy, and follow your commands. Leave unfinished... and GO!

Another tool to have in your arsenal are motivational cards. Some people call them coping cards. I don't like the word 'coping.' It sounds too victim-like, too powerless, and that we aren't... unless we sign on for that. If you are still reading this book you aren't a victim. You don't want pity and neither do I. Motivational cards are for when we are feeling really low or challenged and we want to pick ourselves up. This is where we TAKE A STAND... a RESOLVE. These motivational cards are not designed to make us feel certain. They are designed to make us feel EMPOWERED and what that means is that they are to remind us of these positive principals. So for example, if I am worried about whether God will let me sleep at night, I could go to my motivational card (MY RESOLVE, MY STAND) which would say something like, "I have no idea what or who God really is but what I DO KNOW is that I have been given one life to live to my fullest. When I am on my death bed, I don't want to look back on my life and have regrets and say that I lived my life (my only life) based on fear, worry, and 'what ifs.' I want to make my choices with steadfast courage consistent with what I want, not what my fear or obsession tries to demand. That's all. No thinking past that. No 'what ifs,' no 'what if world.' So your STAND card could say something that would presence you to these principles and remind you of YOUR RESOLVE in that moment of mind freeze... when that moment of anxiety freezes you.

Another tip/insight is to discover the difference between YOU and your OCD... very, very critical. I used to always think they were all one with me. They're not and you need to work at differentiating the two. It is critical in recovery. My OCD is the thing that comes upon me that I don't want to be there. It scares me and kind of has the potential to ruin my day. That's OCD, that's not me. 'Gregg' is more of what I would do if I were not anxious. That's more of who YOU are too. What you choose to do when you're not anxious...your taste in music, foods.... the things you would do in your free time, the things you enjoy, likes and dislikes, the things that are important to you about the world. That is who you are. So that is YOU. That is the genuine YOU. You want to recognize the difference between the time you are spending with the OCD part of you and the time you are spending with the REAL YOU. You want to spend more time in the reality of the actual authentic YOU, not the you that reacts to the fear, obsessions, and anxiety. You want to move from that and say, "How do I CHOOSE to respond to this," not "How do I HAVE TO, or " How MUST I" or " I GOTTA" figure this out, or "I NEED TO." That's all OCD world. But the response when it's YOU is, "I CHOOSE to not spend any time on this. I CHOOSE to move forward while feeling anxious, confused, and uncertain, and to live my life, and "come what may." Yes that's scary and yes that is powerfully taking your STAND. That is YOU. So you want to recognize that difference and follow the REAL YOU which yields tremendous happiness!

I have also discovered how to respond to the crippling, paralyzing question, "How do I know it's OCD, how do I know it's not?" Well, first of all, remember the foundation for getting over OCD is to be uncertain. Accept it and live anyway, regardless of how you feel. So our basic answer, if we are really healthy and on our game, when our minds asks, "How do you know its OCD and not the real thing?" Your response would be, "I don't." That cuts it right there. "Yah, but I feel remarkably anxious if I say that." Exactly, good. We need to feel anxious to get better. Feeling anxious isn't the problem. Not living, not attempting to do something productive while feeling anxious is the problem. "So how do I know if this isn't OCD?" We don't. "Well how do I know when I'm having a panic attack that it isn't a real heart attack and I should go to the doctor?" You don't and you don't need to know if your primary commitment is to recover from OCD, not to not having a heart attack. You have to risk having a heart attack and not getting help for it if you want to recover from OCD. Decide.

What do you want? Are you serious about getting over OCD? How badly do you want it? Are you willing to risk not knowing if it's a heart attack? Are you willing to not respond to the symptoms while not knowing 100 percent for sure what it is? Decide. Don't waste your time trying to get better if you're not. You're wasting your time.

There is another cool insight that I have learned, and again don't try to make this about certainty or absoluteness or you are missing the point of it. According to research, OCD does not mimic reality. So, if you're in the OCD world you might say to yourself, "How do I know it's not reality, not the real thing?" When it is reality you don't have any question as to whether it may be OCD. No question. So when you get shot in the arm... a bullet in your arm... you don't say, "What if this is OCD?" Reality feels nothing like OCD, nothing. So if you think it might be OCD, treat it like it is. That's the approach to take. "Yah, but how do I know for sure it's not a heart attack... yada yada, yada..." you go with that approach to become free of this monster. That is the stance. That is the position you take. We are not trying to find certainty. We are trying to live reasonably... we are trying to break free of OCD. Take a reasonable healthy viewpoint as anyone else would in the world that doesn't have OCD. The point is, if the question even arises, you assume it's OCD. You make the courageous choice if you are in doubt... end of story. No better than that and no worse than that. That is as much as is available to us and every human being on earth and that is enough. That is the treatment and a proper way to deal with it and handle it... very, very important piece.

There is clearly a proven path to recovering from OCD, AND you must be willing to follow that path. The single most important requirement for recovery is that you make recovering from OCD the MOST IMPORTANT thing in your life. I mean that literally. You must be willing to risk that you may act on that obsessive thought in your head that you 'could' molest your child. You take that risk by purposely putting yourself in the company of your child while you are having that horrific thought of "what if I sexually molest her?" What's it gonna be? Are you 100 percent committed to recovering from OCD or are you going to continue playing the 'safe,' 'slave to fear game?' Are you going to continue to deprive yourself and your child of spending time together? You want a guarantee? You got one there. If you continue to give into OCD by avoiding your child when you have that horrific obsessional thought, it is guaranteed that your child will continue to suffer from not having a much-needed relationship with you. You are the PARENT. AVOIDING your child is abuse. There's your guarantee. Being a good person isn't enough. We need RADICAL, AGGRESSIVE COURAGE. So make the only responsible choice and make getting over OCD number one in your life and not ...do not play it 'safe.' The buck stops here, right now, with you. And if you're confused, you're gonna take the risk. That is how you must live. That is the path to take in living your life. That is being a SOLID, COMMITED PARENT. That is the way to go PERIOD.

In wrapping up this chapter, one of the most important tips or strategies is this - be willing to be uncertain and be willing to be uncertain as often as possible. This is the path to freedom from OCD. In conjunction with that - Go after feeling anxious. You want to feel anxious and keep living your life as if you weren't anxious. Is it hard? Yes. Can it be done? Yes. What are the actions you would take if you were not anxious right now? "Yah, but I am." It doesn't matter; you still have the ability to think. In a dreamland, if you weren't anxious right now, what would you choose to do if this problem didn't exist? And that is the healthy action that you take. You go work out. You go write. You go make those business phone calls... you go pay those bills. You don't stay in your head thinking. "Yah, but I feel horrible." It doesn't matter. Be a robot in these moments. Be a good soldier. And the more you do that the sooner relief will find you and OCD will break. Commitment to uncertainty in our daily life and a commitment to high anxiety will ever so steadily move us toward freedom and out of this web and rat wheel that OCD has had us on for far too long. We are choosing to stop it because this is the one life we have... the only life we have! We want to live it to the best of our ability.

When we are on our deathbed looking back, we can say: "You know, I did it the best way I knew how. I did it without FEAR ruling me." " To Thine Own Self Be True" - nothing better. And as a bonus, you leave a legacy for those around you... your friends... your family... your children. You've made your life an example of how to live fully and powerfully, that's what they will always remember you by, and quite possibly they will follow your example in some form or fashion. What a powerful contribution you are making to the world - living your life forward and as powerfully as you can in that moment... in the midst of an anxious, fearful, challenged experience. That is a very powerful message, not only for people with OCD, but for everyone.

CHAPTER FOUR

CHOICES & CONTROL WE HAVE WITH OCD

Okay, so with OCD we tend to focus on what we don't have control over. We don't have control over whether our hands will or won't sweat when we are getting ready to shake someone's hand. We don't have control over whether we sleep well or not. We don't have control over the nature of God, or whether we get a germ or a virus, or when and how we die. We don't have total control over whether something bad happens to our child or not. These things, of course, are fertile grounds for OCD. However the areas that a lot of times we don't focus on, I have learned, are the areas that we do have control over. To focus on what we do have control over is critically important in dealing with and overcoming

OCD. We tend to forget the areas that we have control over because we are focused on the areas that we don't have control over and we do this because those areas that we don't have control over scare the shit out of us. Exposures help stop this stuff from scaring us, making it easier to focus on the areas that we do have control over and that winds up being enough. That's when the areas that we don't have control over no longer have that horrifying, crippling impact on us. As a result, we can live a happy, peaceful, fruitful, productive, empowered life.

To Compulse or Not

One area that we have control over is whether we compulse or not, albeit difficult at times. Compulsing takes our approval... our permission for us to do our ritual... for us to respond to the obsession that comes to us by trying to make ourselves feel better. So if I'm driving down the road and I see a 17 on a license plate, the thought hits me, "Oh that's quite a coincidence, I was just thinking about religion. That must mean that I have to be Catholic." That's the obsession. I have no control over whether that pops into my head or not. However, I do have control over whether I try to negate that thought, or engage or debate that thought in order to make myself feel better - which is the compulsion - which is the ritual - which is the 'figuring out' compulsion. I have control over whether I do that or not and I have control over whether I just let that be there and let it make me anxious and continue living anyway. I do have control. If someone had a gun to my head and said, "If you try to make this go away I will shoot you," I would most likely, not try to make it go away. Or if somebody said, "If you can try to just let that be there and not intentionally try to make it better or go away for the next 8 minutes, I will give you $10,000,000 dollars in cash," I could most likely do it. These seem like extreme examples, however it does prove the point that we do have control over whether we compulse or not.

Another area that we have control over is that we can CHOOSE (powerful word) to DISOBEY OCD. We can. OCD will say, "Don't step on that crack or something bad is going to happen to your child." As difficult as it is to choose to purposely disobey OCD and step on that crack, you CAN do it. You might say, "Oh my God, well that's killing my child,"... really? You definitely don't know that. But you do know that you have the power (the physical ability) to disobey OCD... to step on that crack. Your leg can physically rise in the air and your foot can place itself right down on that crack and you can put all your weight on it. You have the physical power to do that. I'm not talking about how it feels. I'm talking about whether you have the physical ability to do that and yes you do. In this area we have control. We can disobey OCD. This is the core of our recovery.

Another area that we have control over, and it kind of goes together with the first area about not compulsing, is that when the obsession hits us, in whatever form it comes: a feeling, a thought, an image, an impulse - whatever it comes in, we can choose to do one of two healthy things. We can choose to either do what we are supposed to be doing in the moment, or we can choose to do an exposure. If you are driving and the thought comes to you, some obsessive thought, you can choose to just continue driving. You can increase your focus on driving. "What am I supposed to be doing right now?

What should I be doing right now? Oh, that's right, I'm driving. I'm not supposed to be going off in 'lala' land in my head." You can refocus on driving with more intention and focus. Look at the lines, make sure you are in the middle of the lane, look forward, and watch your speed, check and see, really focus on driving. That is in your control. That is a choice you can make. It's in your power. You CAN choose that. You CAN choose to respond by simply not doing the compulsion, staying in the moment, and saying to yourself, "What am I supposed to be doing right now? Oh yeah that's right, I'm eating. Chew and taste more. Let me focus on eating and being more aware... get into the details, put more awareness and more intention on my eating. Even though the obsession is still trying to break through, don't intentionally engage in it. Even if it does break through and makes you feel bad, keep going back to focusing on eating. Keep going back to focusing on driving. And/or we can choose to do an exposure and make it 'worse' which, as we know, ultimately makes things better. That power is in our hands with OCD.

We also have the power that when we feel completely fearful, burdened, overwhelmed, and belittled by OCD, we have the power to keep our legs moving. This is a very powerful metaphor for me when I'm doing exposures and I've got my headset on and I'm walking. No matter how anxious I feel, or depressed, or down, or how off I am, I can choose to keep my legs moving... one leg at a time. It's a powerful metaphor and it could be a powerful one for you as well...keeping the legs moving no matter how horrible you feel, you can still put one leg in front of the other - a robotic type motion - and continue moving forward. And it is that 'continuing to move' that will bring you out of it. You know the saying, "When you are going through hell, keep moving." Very, very, true and powerful adage.

The other control that we have is that we can choose to look for OCD, to look for things that will make us obsess (spike hunts.) We can choose to welcome it and we can choose to try and increase the anxiety, and then hope for it to stay. We truly do have the control and power to make those crazy choices. We do, ultimately. And it is those crazy choices that bring us out of this.

Feels like a crazy condition why not have a crazy treatment?!!

The other choice we have is we can carry a blank index card in our pocket with a little golf pencil or pen... always looking for the next obsession. We're not running from it. We are looking for it and when it comes to us, we can grab it and put it down on a card... we have our next exposure, our next access to freedom. When we do that, the obsessions will come less and less because OCD runs away when we run towards it. When we run away, it chases us, and gets more powerful... very powerful, powerful information right there. Remember little nuances and insights such as: 'embrace the anxiety,' 'lighten up,' 'keep moving,' 'let the house burn down,' which means that when our amygdala is sending us a five alarm fire alert and we get that urgent, fight or flight feeling, we can choose to stay there and let the house burn down. We can choose to memorize and write down this powerful notion on the cards we carry, 'COMMIT EMOTIONAL SUICIDE' every time OCD confronts us. Getting over OCD is being willing to commit what FEELS like emotional suicide over and over and over and over again. We can choose to do this over and over again. That is what it takes to get over OCD. This is what it takes to takes to TAKE BACK YOUR LIFE!

Now, we will have to remind ourselves of these principles because they don't come naturally. It's not natural to want to put ourselves through what appears to be misery. However, it is absolutely that training of our mind and spirit... the motivation to want to go into the lion's den... that brings us out of the depths OCD and depression. So, we can choose to remind ourselves of these principles and to embed them in our brains until they become second nature, by memorizing, carrying around cards, putting them around the house, anything like that. That is a skill that we need to learn, even though it is counter intuitive to our reasoning, in order to get over OCD. We can post it in places that we see often: our nightstand by our bed, the mirror in the bathroom, the kitchen refrigerator, the dash board in the car. All of these little, incredibly significant things we can do. We can CHOOSE to do these things. This is powerful. And when we choose to do these things and we start doing them, we will find out that the things that we don't have direct control over don't have as much impact or punch. Because when we are choosing to do the things that we are in our control of like exercising (which is critical in managing OCD and depression,) when we're doing those things and we're eating right and we are continuing to move forward... even if it is much slower, in that difficult moment of choice by keeping our legs moving forward no matter how lousy we feel, when we are doing that, our self- esteem goes up, we feel better, our level of confidence goes up and we realize, "Hey, I don't have to have complete and total certainty in order to be productive, and fulfilled and happy in my life." All we have to do is to continue moving forward at whatever pace (important not to be critical here about your performance) and to continue focusing on the things that we do have control over, such as reminding ourselves that moving towards the anxiety is the safest place. Then the obsession loses its impact. Let's go there and make it our goal every day, moment by moment, to go there starting right now... move towards the anxiety! I'm in. How 'bout you?

CHAPTER FIVE

EXAMPLE OF OBSESSION & STEP-BY-STEP RESPONSE

So let's take the following obsession of mine: I'm getting ready to go out to a party in the evening and all of a sudden the obsession, the thought, the feeling comes to me and says, "Now you know it's important that you look at these people the right way and look at them in the eyes." And then immediately, since I know this obsession so well, my anxiety and my thoughts will go to, "Okay, wait a minute, how do I do that?" But, of course, it's not something you do. It's just involuntary. Your eyes do what they do. You look someone's way and that's all. You don't break it down, but nonetheless, there's an urgency that tells me I have to. "Okay, so what are you going to do now?! Oh my God, you don't know how to look at somebody... you're gonna... it's going to be horrible tonight!" I feel the anxiety well up inside of me. The first thing to do is to remind myself of 'don't just do something, stand there' (very good phrase for me.) No thinking or panicking or ritualizing, instead STAND there. "You're gonna look like an idiot if you don't know how to look at people. Nobody's gonna talk to you, you're gonna look weird. They're gonna be wondering why you're not looking the right way in their eyes, nobody's gonna... you're not gonna have any friends, you're not gonna be successful, your family is gonna starve, and you are going to have a horrible life and be depressed! You have to figure out how to do this before tonight!" Do nothing. Next, choose to not panic. Panic means you have chosen and lost control. Next, hold the feeling and hang out there with it. Feel the anxiety associated with that concern about looking at someone at the party. Then say, "I want this. I want this anxiety right now. This is where I need to be to get better." That's how you welcome it. That's how you accept it. That's how you embrace it. "Good, I'm glad this feeling and concern are here. I know that when I get anxious and I'm willingly allowing it, that's when I'm getting better, I'm getting stronger. Good deal." Your #1 priority in your life is GETTING OVER OCD...FREEDOM. It is not going to the party tonight free of anxiety. The other thing to remember as you go through this is that your anxiety is not the gauge of how serious the matter is.

It is very important to pay attention to the response that we have to the symptom or feeling or thought, not the actual symptom, feeling, or thought itself (Dr. Reed Wilson). You don't want your response to be a PANICKY, anxious one such as, "Oh my God! I'm feeling tense. I'm feeling tight; I'm feeling.... people are going to think I'm crazy tonight by how I look. I am going to be embarrassed and humiliated." You want to focus more on accepting it. Pay attention to if you are saying, "Good, I'm glad this is here. This is where I need to be to get better." I have captured this distressing, 'unacceptable' feeling or thought because I know that by hanging out in this awful feeling or letting the horrible thought be there I am getting used to this panic, fear, and distress and once we get used to this feeling it will stop bothering us and our problem becomes solved. This is the path to freedom. "I am glad I captured this. "HOLD." HANG OUT there a bit. This is the exposure. This is the path to freedom. I knew this to be true before trying it because the professionals who are on the cutting edge of OCD research said so and I decided to put my faith in that and in the treatment and REALLY try it...no bullshit, feeble attempt. I know it's true now because I have done it. You don't have to take my word for it but if you want to get better you have to put your faith in the treatment and try it. What the hell do you have to lose? Stop protecting yourself and get well. Refuse to run from this any longer. Are you choosing to hang out in that feeling or are you running scared in fear, praying for mercy to make that horrible feeling or thought go away? That's the defining moment. There is nothing wrong with praying as long as it is backed up with good, solid, bold action. Feebleness and feeling sorry for yourself will not get you over OCD. Audacious, volitional intent, moving towards capturing the feeling we have hated for so long and hanging out in it until it no longer bothers us, will. This is difficult but far from impossible. It becomes easier and easier by consistently recognizing it as "the moment of choice." That moment is waiting for our response and that response determines whether the chains of OCD are loosening or tightening. The more we resist and run from it scared, the tighter they get. Don't take the bait for immediate gratification by trying to make ourselves feel better in the moment...by thinking through the obsession or some other compulsion we do. We want to let ourselves feel bad but continue to do good. This is very important in recovering from OCD and depression. Allow yourself to feel bad but to do good and allow your performance to be diminished. Never judge it. Come aboard and fight for your freedom as I and many before you have. You won't be disappointed.

In dealing with an obsession (a thought we don't want, a feeling we don't want, whatever you want to call it,) it is important that we take the offensive strategy. It is important to do the opposite of trying to make ourselves feel better in the moment. It's kind of like, if we are depressed, what might feel better in the moment is to go lay down and that's probably not the path to take. Calling a friend, taking a walk, or working out would be much better options which may be the last thing we want to do.

It is the same with OCD. We don't want to try to make ourselves feel better in the moment... by thinking through the obsession or compulsing some other way. We don't want to do that. We want to take the offensive strategy. We want to let ourselves feel bad but continue to do good. This is very important in recovering from OCD and depression. Allow ourselves to feel bad but to do good and allow for our performance to be diminished.

We can also go with the 'act as if' strategy. Act as if you feel good and then do good and see what happens. You very well may feel better, even good possibly. Your whole world could change for you as a result of doing good action when you don't feel good. Try it. There is something waiting for you at the other end.

It really is about asserting ourselves over our feelings. This is established in our being. Who's in control, us or our feelings? When we do assert ourselves over the present feeling by taking action good feelings will show up. They will show up later but not before. The way it works is that we have to 'DO' first and THEN we 'GET' happiness, not the other way around. When we feel our absolute worst and there is nothing in us for a work out, that's when we really, really benefit from driving to the gym and seeing what happens. This is that leap of faith. This is where faith and trust come in. We don't get a return on our investment until we invest in it. There is a return on our investment when we invest wisely... healthy ACTION is always a wise investment. This kind of work is to be done every day, moment by moment, not by once choosing to do this and then for the rest of our lives that's it. No. It is a moment-by-moment CHOICE and ONLY A MOMENT-BY-MOMENT CHOICE. Don't make it less than that and not do it, and don't make it more than that and burn out and stop doing it. Our 'choice' in every moment will determine if we take the easy way, the unhealthy way, or if we take what appears to be the difficult, challenged way, the healthy way, and the path... the way out of OCD and into a free, happy life. So it's important to work towards that as difficult as it may be. It is also important to take it in manageable sizes. MOVE, DO, HANG OUT in the feeling, ACT as if you feel good and confident.

Be aware of the unhealthy responses to OCD: 'Watch out,' 'move away,' 'this is annoying,' 'oh my God this is horrible,' 'avoid,' 'fight,' 'run,' 'brace,' 'change this,' 'get comfortable,' 'play it safe.' Those are the responses to OCD that do not benefit us. That is when OCD is dominating and winning. So if I am having an obsession that my voice could sound weird and that makes me self-conscious about my timing when I speak or make a joke and I start to think, "What if the devil has possessed me and I don't sound funny, or good, or cool?" And then I literally start to sound that way to myself. Well, the unhealthy way to respond to that is to say, "Well I gotta convince myself that it isn't true and that my voice really does sound good. Or I gotta change the way I feel and make sure my voice is going to sound relaxed, pleasing, and motivating to people. Then I'm going to watch for people's responses to see if I'm still funny and likable, or if my timing is off because I am now paying attention to this. I'm gonna keep my eye on this and I'm going to control this. I gotta control how I sound, and look, and come off"… wrong way!! I am losing. OCD is DOMINATING!!!

When we are winning is when we are putting caution to the wind. "I'm just gonna talk and look at people how I want to. I'm going to do my thing and make jokes and whatever and enjoy myself and not worry about others (to sing like no one is listening and to dance like no one is watching.) Let it land where it may. Let the shit fall where it may. Yah, but if you do that and, you know, you've lost your timing and could be possessed by the devil or something, and you're no longer funny because you're self-conscious, you may get embarrassed and people may hate you and you may no longer make a living and you will be lonely, alone, depressed all your life... who wants to be with a devil-ridden dude who sounds weird and isn't funny!" Wow!! The response to that is, "Bring it and we'll see." As hard as that is, then get up and MOVE and go DO SOMETHING positive. Don't sit and worry and obsess. Do push-ups, take a walk, work on your book, pay some bills, move, do your taxes, clear off and organize your desk or closet or garage or basement, or wash your car, or call someone lonely, or write a kind letter to someone, or pet or brush your dog. Have a written list of things you can do and carry it with you. "I am responsible for my effort not the result if I am well received by others. I am responsible for not trying to change or control how my voice sounds in the moment. It is my responsibility to MODEL how to respond to OCD when it shows itself, NOTHING ELSE. My #1 commitment in my life is to recovering from OCD. It is not to be a fantastic speaker. Recovering from OCD always trumps speaking well. It must be this way when being challenged by OCD.

Also, when you feel that negative thought, feeling, urge, sensation - the response to have is, "I want uncertainty. Good. I want this. I am staying here. This is where I want to be. Yah but I'm scared! I WANT to be SCARED." You won't feel strong or good in this spot, but this is the spot to be. It's necessary to get better. This is the place where you have to show courage. You keep it, hold it, and make intentional choices that are healthy while you are feeling this and say, "We'll see." You're dominating!! You're winning when you feel like you're losing! Choosing to stay there, not to wallow in it, but to allow yourself to feel bad and to do things that are productive while you are feeling bad… difficult work. It takes a lot of practice and a lot of repetition. It seems like an absurd position to take, but stay with this and hold there against your will. Let yourself be scared and embrace and accept that and say, " I want this." It seems absurd and yet it is the path out of this. You have to tie a knot and hang on and continue to try, try, try, try, with this stuff. It is a process. It is a discovery. This is second by second work. The responses that we have are very subtle but the impact is major. How we respond to the OCD, the anxiety, the discomfort, the fear, the concern, the feeling... our mind is watching and it is recognizing and observing whether we are viewing this as critical and terrifying or not. And if we are avoiding, being scared, trying to alter our feeling in that moment, running, fighting and giving in, then our brain is going to continue to give it to us because it will then believe, by our response to it, that this is important to us. We are giving it significance. We have to not give it relevance even though it sucks at times. We have to continue through it, have faith in the treatment and not let that moment rule us!

Give yourself a week or two to try this stuff. Or two days and say, "I'm not gonna pay attention to this bad shit and I'm just gonna keep on trying to muscle my way through, keep doing good, and 'act as if' and see what happens. A good strong motivator is, "I want my life back! I want my freaking life back!" This requires choosing to willingly go through a period of uncertainty and suckiness. That's not fun, but the prize you get is your LIFE and HAPPINESS. Keep your eye on the PRIZE when you are doing this work and your life and your happiness will be yours. Suck it up for now.

We have to remember that what we want is COURAGE. We're not going after confidence. The difference between these two is critical in recovering from OCD. Confidence is your hands not shaking, your voice not quivering or stuttering. Courage is having your hands shake and tolerating people noticing it and continuing to live your life with passion and purpose. We are going after our hands shaking, not trying to hide it, and tolerating people noticing it. How 'bout that? Let it all hang out. We're not trying to come off cool and good. We are talking about increasing our tolerance and our resilience for embarrassment... our tolerance for discomfort and our tolerance for what we think other people are thinking about us. That's their problem man. Just do your job. Just continue with your EFFORT and your ACTION in the moment of what you are doing. What would you do if you felt good? Then do that. Go with that. See how that goes for a week without questioning it and asking all kinds of safe questions... which gets you nowhere.

The three best words in responding to an OCD question are, 'I don't know.' Are we resisting or are we saying, "This is good, this is a good time to practice. This sucks and it is good because my freedom starts when I feel bad and I allow it." We have to feel bad in order to get good. So when we feel bad, even though we don't like it, we have to remind ourselves that this is an opportunity to stop the buck here and practice and hang out in this feeling of uncertainty and distress at this moment. Just let it be there and feel it. Hang out in it. Hold on and see what happens. Don't figure it out. Don't play it safe. Take risks and live what feels to be very, very dangerous. Bring it close - that feeling - and hold it, that horrible feeling, and keep going. It takes tremendous effort and fortitude. And the best way to get there is not all at once but through practice and continuing over and over and over in trying to recommit and not looking for that place of comfort, security, and ease. We can't go there man!

We need to also remember to change the language in our mind. The OCD language and the language that is ineffective and makes our condition worse is, "If I don't figure this out, I could be screwed forever." That's very difficult to tolerate in a moment. So we want to change our language in our mind to this, when that moment hits, "If I don't figure this out, I will feel very anxious and that is good for me now and I can handle that." That's the language! Work on changing that. We get there by repetition… practice, practice, and practice.

Our job is to purposely bring on more anxiety and uncertainty than we think we can handle in the moment. Wow, that sucks right? Kind of, until you start doing it and you get on a wave with it moment by moment. It's moment-by-moment work. Bring on anxiety and uncertainty and feel it and feel more than you think you can tolerate and see what happens. We have to break this.

We have to break this bitch, and this bitch is in us. A part of us has got to break. And that's when we win! The work is moment by moment by moment... practice, practice, practice, practice, practice! That is what will get you there. I know. I have done it and continue to. You can too. All you have to do is start it. Don't stop and you will see what I'm talking about. Never feel bad about yourself... only feel good about recommitting to trying again and again and again!

We also have to remember to educate ourselves and to learn what it takes to get better, to presence ourselves to these principles daily, numerous times a day. Keep them by your nightstand. Study. Read. You're changing your entire way of thinking. This is big work and requires a lot of it and "my, my" is it rewarding. Remember that when we are tired or we don't feel well, or our allergies are flaring, or our sinuses are bad, and we feel vulnerable, defenseless, awkward, clumsy, off our game, or scared... remember this principal - use courage and act like a robot. Just do the treatment. That's the time you will be most challenged is when you feel off your game for whatever reason, you're not feeling it. You don't have to be feeling it to do it. This work doesn't require feeling it. It only requires doing it, showing up. And we think because we feel bad and we don't feel real good while we are doing it that we are missing something, something's wrong. No! Something is right! Keep presensing yourself to that principal. Something's right when you're not feeling like it's going right. That's when it's right. You just hang in there and mother #!?X%!! DO it. Make it take you out before you stop doing it and see what happens, and don't project into the future what's gonna happen. Just KEEP GOING man. Live what feels like to be CRAZY and IRRESPONSIBLE by not checking and fixing. Practice, practice, practice... and remind yourself that when this stuff hits, you're gonna welcome it. You're gonna take it, you're not gonna chase it away. You're gonna say, "Okay here it is, if I don't do this I'm gonna feel anxious and I can handle that and it's good for me now, for sure it is." Have faith in the treatment all the way through recovery. Do exposures when you are struggling and keep moving.

We need to program ourselves and we need to continue moving forward. The only way OCD can take you out is if you say it has. So if you are alive, not blown away, or taken out, continue your movements and healthy responses to the feelings and thoughts you don't want until there is no breath left in your body. The response you want is acceptance and a continuation of moving forward and acting as if you felt better as evidenced by the choices you make. Pay attention to the response you have to the feeling instead of the 'feeling' so much. Say to yourself, "I'm taking my life back. Take me down if you want, you #?+!**. I'm taking my life back. Take me down if you want. You #@!?*. Because I'm not stopping until that **%#!?+!! happens." That is MOMENT-BY-MOMENT COMMITTMENT. Start doing it RIGHT NOW! Whatever you are afraid of right now, challenge it. Right now! And remember to say to yourself and proclaim, "Good, this is where I need to be and where I want to be. I'm getting better when I'm personally willing to be in this uncomfortable place. I want to be anxious, uncomfortable, scared, confused, vulnerable, defenseless, awkward, clumsy, down." Remind yourself of that statement when you're feeling tired and off-your-game and then say, "Oh, okay, I want to feel this. This is a good chance for me to practice and continue growing. Then when I get better I'm gonna be that much better because I'm going through this hard time right now." No one may know you're kickin' ass but down deep you know you are and that's all you need. When you feel like shit and you say, "I wanna be anxious, and 'off' and you don't look like you're doing great but you make that proclamation and you embrace that reality that you are experiencing in that moment, you are studin' out. No one knows it but you, down deep, and when your mind and your OCD tries to object by saying, " Yah, but what if this continues forever?" Your response is, "Whatever." That's it and you stay in your moment... very important stuff. Remember that when you feel challenged that is your opportunity to demonstrate that you are not going to let the anxiety, fear, confusion... whatever you are feeling... determine what you are doing next. No longer are you going to allow it to pull you around by the short hairs. You're taking risks. You're taking that leap. You are jumping in. You are diving in. YOU ARE TAKING YOUR LIFE BACK. That is what will break this.

This isn't for the faint of heart and if you are faint of heart, continue practicing and recommitting anyway.

Don't stop trying. This work that I talk about is not easy AND it is very effective. Some people say, "Well, what if a lot of people aren't willing to do this?" That's their choice. This is what has made me better. I want to talk to that one person out there who is willing to do this work. It's not a feel good therapy. It doesn't have to be AND there is freedom at the end. If there's one of you out there that feels you're ready - not even if you're ready - but if you're willing to take the plunge, that's who I'm here for. We are not trying to make that moment easier. We want the moment to be unabated. We don't want to encumber it with comfort. Let it be what it is. Take it as it comes. Keep going until you're taken out. That's all you're responsible for. You're not responsible for anything else... so, whatever. Got it? You're not responsible for you coming off funny or your voice sounding good or your timing being good. No, you're responsible for doing your stuff and allowing for the uncomfortable feelings and thoughts to be there, NO MATTER HOW MUCH THEY SCARE THE SHIT OUT OF YOU. CONTINUE with it anyway and to allow for diminished capacity... to allow for your performance to not be the best. To recognize that you're probably gonna feel anxious if you allow it, and you can you handle that. Can you really not handle this one second longer? Can you really not take it one second longer? Really? No, it's not true. It doesn't have to feel fantastic or wonderful when you're trying to get better. You can do what you have to do. Just keep it up and it will crack. It will break. The shell of OCD will crack and you will come through it. The access to that is when the times are tough, keep moving until you're taken out, even if you're not doing well... even if you don' think that you're doing a good job. It's not about that. It's continuing to show up and staying with that moment that is delivered, however it is delivered, unabated. Continue moving forward and living - no matter the condition you're in or how you feel or how screwed up you think you are or how you are doing when you are in that moment and trying to move forward. And it's continuing to risk. When you're putting your ego on the line... when you are putting yourself on the line risking embarrassment, loneliness and rejection... when you're putting that on the line, you're really doing well. Even if it seems like it is going badly, the answer is to continue to risk rejection and continue to put it on the line over and over and over again. It won't last forever. It will crack, if you keep doing it. You gotta do it. It's that emotional suicide piece. You gotta do it! You CAN do it. I have and continue to and you can too. Do what you know to do.

CHAPTER SIX

THE MOMENT OF CHOICE

THE MOMENT of choice is that moment when you're tired, scared, and you go anyway. It takes a lot of strength, commitment, courage, and conviction to go when you feel like this. That's the moment of choice. When somebody asks, "Well, can you handle it?" And your honest response is, "I don't know but I'm going anyway." That's when you're kickin' ass. It's that moment of choice, manifested in so many different ways. It's that moment that determines if we are going to improve or not. It's that moment that determines if we are living our lives so as to have no regrets. Let that be your motivation to make the tough choices again and again and again. It's that moment when we decide if we are jumping back in bed or flipping on the TV or leaving the house and 'going' that determines if we are winning at life or not. You may or may not notice the benefit right away, but you will notice it very soon. And we have to always remember, that if we work a little harder today, it will make living easier tomorrow. Well, that means we gotta get off it about feeling good right now. Suck it up... do it for tomorrow. We're doing the work now so we can gain more later. Okay. It's called emotional maturity. It's called commitment. It's an investment. It's called moving towards a goal. It's not easy. Remember what to do when it's not easy... when you're feeling that. Pay attention to how you are responding to it and that you're not trying to run from it... that you're still following through with your healthy choices. That's the deal. Commit (what feels like) Emotional Suicide and risk as often... as often as possible, moment-by-moment, second by second. Rejection - you want to risk it. Are people gonna accept you because your palms are sweaty? You gotta risk it and do it anyway. The fear can't silence you if you refuse to allow it. It can't. You are where you are right now, and you're gonna do what you can do right now and then you'll see what happens... period. Move through. It can be dark... heavy dark. You can't see, but you can choose to continue to move in the face of uncertainty. You may not know if you're gonna fall, if you're gonna stumble, or what. And you can STILL CHOOSE to continue to move forward. That's THE MOMENT OF CHOICE. That's what I mean when I say 'STAND.' When you're so beat up by this stuff and you feel that you have nothing left, say to yourself, 'STAND.' Let that be your resolve (mantra) and always STAND UP no matter how weak you feel. STAND and CONTINUE. Be a good soldier. Let it happen BUT do your part and remember what your part is in those challenging moments. Your part is to remind yourself of what you would do if you felt good right now and go do it even though you are feeling compromised. That's it man. Go for that. Go for that. Suck it up. Take it on.

When you feel your worst and you're scared and you're doing your worst but you're still doing, have faith that that's when you're winning. Go with it. Try it for a night and see what happens. Why seek certainty instead of living? Let's live! Right? I mean, you still have a choice. I don't know if the devil has possessed me or could possess me or will possess me or not. One thing I do know is that I have the choice to continue moving forward and to continue putting forth my EFFORT. I do have that choice. As long as I have that I'm not shuttin' up and I'm not worrying about feeling good. I'm just gonna keep on goin' and allowing for diminished capacity and doing the best to the best of my ability, and that's it. Let someone else take me out. I'm not. That's all. And don't try to figure it out. Just go. Just go. Now. Okay. I'll go now. Let's do it!

Accept the reality of where you are. Accept it as it comes. Let it be there. Move with it. Stay in it and continue going and work towards a better tomorrow with this... and do exposures. Make yourself scared. You just need to bask in the anxiety. Feel that feeling over and over and over again until it no longer bothers you... until you're just bored with it and you just want to get on with things one way or another. That's the place of freedom. That's the place of complete and total disregard for something negative happening. And you reach that place by hanging out in the anxiety that feels so bad. Make room for it. Relentlessly hang on at this moment. IT

WILL BREAK... ALWAYS DOES IF YOU CAN HOLD. I can, others do, and with practice, SO CAN YOU!

It's not about controlling whether you blush, vomit, or stutter. It's about removing the fear of that happening and that people will reject you. How do you do that? You do that by taking that risk (over and over again) that your fear could happen. Expose yourself to the thought that you could be possessed and that you could sound weird, everybody hates you and you could be miserable, alone and depressed for the rest of your life. Get rid of the fear of that. Remember to live and die moving. Follow your commands. Go from being imprisoned to being free and the way you do that is to accept the imprisonment until it runs out. You are not running from this. You are running to it. Powerfully choose to do that and to maintain your DIGNITY by not giving up and facing it head on often. It will retreat. Risk equals freedom. "How ya choosin'?" not "How ya feelin?"

OCD and DIGNITY is a powerful concept. Your dignity is about your effort. That's what it's about. It's about continuing in your life and your recovery until you time runs out. Period. We don't want to be certainty junkies. We want to live with risk versus trying to find certainty which stops us from living. Make it worse. Avoid the 'what if?' trap. Our actions define who we are. Let OCD take its shots at you. Just do a tiny part. Just give 1% when it's tough, but give that 1%. This is where it's at! Commit and drive to the gym when you feel lousy. See what happens. That's the 1% and that is enough. TRUST IT and TRY IT.

We have covered numerous topics related to OCD. There's understanding OCD. There are the exposures… critical. There are our choices and the control we have and what we don't have. There's a series of events and how to move through an obsessive moment. There are commands. There's the idea of powerful living. That is a whole other book with or without OCD. Powerful living is what we're talking about doing here. It's not a feeling. It's a choice, that's all. We covered strength in weakness… feeling like crap and not quitting, not judging ourselves and allowing things to be there that come to our mind… the 'what ifs,' doing exposures when you need to and going unready, going into the lion's den, asking yourself in the moment, "WHAT CHOICE DO I HAVE RIGHT NOW?" In the action moment... in the moment when it is happening, in that OCD moment, what is my CHOICE?

The choice is to continue until there is no more. That's all. Make room for it (the obsession), let it stay there, invite it to stay, then continue living and doing your life (cut wood, carry water) while you are allowing it to be present. It is critical to really get that. It is HUGE in recovery. Say, "Okay, let's see how bad this can get"... gotta cross that line and go into it bold not fragile. Let's see how bad it can take me out... come on! It's the removal of the fear of the thing happening, not the possibility of the thing happening, that we focus on first. The fear of the possibility of the thing happening, that's the only thing OCD can do to us. That's where we go...ultimate goal versus immediate relief and then we'll see. Don't figure it out and project in the future. "We'll see." Live POWERFULLY by DOING. Don't put your focus and attention on feeling it.

CHAPTER SEVEN

LOVED ONES: DO'S & DON'TS

Living with a person with OCD can be very difficult and confusing. They are in pain, you want to help them. Simple, right? Wrong. You have to go against your nature in order to be helpful to a loved one living with OCD. We want to open the door for them or tie their shoes so they don't have to... re-wash their hands again. We want to tell them that they really are safe in taking their prescribed medication and that it won't accidentally poison them. We want to reassure them that the windows and doors are locked so they can be at peace and get some sleep for the night. True to form, the way to respond to OCD is not how we think we should. It's much closer to the opposite. When he or she asks you if their hands are clean enough so they can stop washing them, reassuring them by saying, "Yes they are clean enough" actually exacerbates the whole problem. The reason this happen is because of the nature of obsessions and compulsions. When they give into the obsession and ask if their hands are clean enough (the asking of the question is the compulsion) and when we answer it and reassure them... this may cause temporary relief for them but the answering of their OCD question actually feeds the OCD cycle. It guarantees they will feel the need to ask the question again when the doubt returns, which it definitely will now. You have just conditioned your loved one that to deal with this doubting obsession that they are experiencing, they must continue to compulsively ask the question enough times until they feel certain and safe again in that moment. Remember, going after certainty and safety causes OCD to grow and spiral out of control.

There are various ways that you can respond to your loved one when they are scared and ask you for reassurance. One way to do this is that when they ask you the obsessive question tell them that you love them too much to contribute to this OCD and you refuse to make it worse for them in the long run by answering. Don't reassure or pity them, instead EMPOWER them. Tell them that this OCD which is causing them to ask the question, is DESTROYING their LIFE and you REFUSE to stand by and watch and CONTRIBUTE to it getting worse because you love them too much. Remind them in that moment what the therapeutic thing is for them and for you to do. It is to live with the uncertainty and the ensuing anxiety that accompanies it by not answering the question and then not continuing to ask it. Rather, leave it hanging and take a risk. Encourage them to never do another compulsion again and tell them you believe in them and you know they can do it. You know they can fight. You know they can get angry at the OCD and refuse to take it anymore.

Remind yourself how OCD works. OCD basically says, "If you don't wash your hands, I will punch you in the stomach." What it doesn't tell you is that if you do wash your hands, it may not punch you right then but it will punch you many times later, eventually to the point of ultimate immobilization and confinement to your bed and room for the rest of your life. It doesn't tell you that in the obsessive moment. The correct response is, "Well, I am definitely not washing my hands and you have to do what you have to do OCD. That is not my business." The reason you respond this way is because you are too smart now to fall for this because you know it is far better to take 1) punch in the stomach now than (5) tomorrow (which it won't tell you but will happen.)

So for those of you watching the one you love suffer, I have some very good and helpful ADVICE. Good and helpful for them and for yourself as a bonus. Teach them how to 'suffer better.' Teach them to accept the discomfort by encouraging them to stay with it and not let discomfort make their choices for them or rule their life. This momentary suffering is their direct path to freedom. Remind them that the discomfort is temporary but recovery from OCD (Freedom) is permanent. Lead your own life according to this as an example for them. You may not have OCD but you do have good and bad feelings and choices to be made during both. Make positive healthy choices when you don't feel good or positive. Model for them how to accept the discomfort of the moment and still do the healthy action, such as going to exercise when you feel tired. By doing this you show them that you aren't ruled by your feelings and emotions but rather by your CHOICES to live a POWERFUL, FULFILLED, DYNAMIC life, as you want them to. Walk it first in your own life and THEN encourage them. They will know the difference. The greatest impact you can have on your loved one with OCD is showing them by your PERSONAL EXAMPLE, moment by moment, day by day, how to live a dynamic, active life. This will get them better quicker than reasoning away their obsession with them or helping them with their rituals, or the opposite, yelling at them for not standing up to it. You first have to stand up to your daily challenges by what you DO, not what you say. If you want them to do the hard work, YOU DO IT FIRST. EMPOWER them, never pity them. Don't make it easy on them to live their OCD life. Mix it up. Be a THORN in their side. It has to get bad enough in order for them to make a CHANGE. Constantly helping and saving them leaves them POWERLESS and MISERABLE.

CHAPTER EIGHT

FINAL BREATH

Okay, OCD brothers and sisters, you have what it takes to OVERCOME OCD. Whether you choose to do it or not is up to YOU. Who's willing? Who's willing to commit what feels like emotional suicide in order to BREAK THE CHAINS of OCD? I am. Come on. Don't take it any longer. Be willing to DIE TRYING and you will win. I have done it and continue to do it. IT WORKS. Your ONLY JOB is to REMOVE the unwanted fear-type feeling that you get when you are prompted or triggered by your specific issue. Do not fall for the TRAP of trying to fix the problem and finding CERTAINTY in your concern. No. Wrong road! The right road is to work at no longer having that unwanted feeling when your obsession shows itself. Don't fix the obsession. Do Not. So, how do you get rid of the UNWANTED FEELING when the obsession hits? First step is to leave the obsession alone. Let it do what it wants for as long as it wants. The second step is to purposely BRING ON your particular obsession as often as possible so that you can feel that awful feeling it provokes as OFTEN as possible. This is part of the process of 'removing the fear' (HABITUATION) you feel from your obsession, (not removing the obsession)... JUST THE FEAR. It is enough. Trust me. Hell, try it and see. The more you bring on and FEEL (purposely) that horrible fear feeling that you don't want, the sooner you will habituate to it and you will be FREE of that problem. I know. I do it. So can you! FEELING the unwanted feeling that your obsession brings burns the feeling out and kills it. Feel it a lot as often as possible. This fear WILL LEAVE on its own when your mind and central nervous system are no longer freaked out by it. You won't have to ask it to leave. It will magically leave if you feel it to the point of BOREDOM... to the point of no longer reacting to it. It's like diving into a fairly cold swimming pool which causes you discomfort. The way to get rid of the discomfort is to STAY in the pool until it NO LONGER FEELS cold to you. Is the water still a problem for you? No. You are FREE of that as a problem. The water temperature didn't change. You FELT IT TO DEATH. You killed the discomfort by feeling it until it was no longer uncomfortable. You didn't work at trying to change the water temperature (your obsession); you didn't DEPRIVE yourself of LIVING by staying out of the pool. No. You knew when to get out of the water.. when it no longer bothered you. You BECAME FREE. You know when to stop your exposure... when the obsession (water) no longer bothers you.

As the story goes, Batman was AFRAID of bats as a result of an unfortunate experience in childhood. He DECIDED he WANTED to OVERCOME THAT FEAR of bats. So he WENT INTO a cave full of them. The COMMAND he gave himself was to STAY in that cave until he was no longer afraid. He COMMITTED to the fear, leaving before he did. He knew when it was time to leave the cave, as do we. This is what we are CALLED TO DO IN RECOVERY. Do you want recovery? Do you want your life back? How badly do you want YOUR LIFE back? How bad do you want it? Make the CHOICE and do not look back! You must be WILLING to RISK it all. I'm telling you, if you are, you WILL WIN your life back. You still have to take your leap of faith and GO INTO THE LION'S DEN. You HAVE TO commit what FEELS like EMOTIONAL SUICIDE and be WILLING to do it OVER and OVER again until the bats (which are still there) no longer bother you. SUCCESS IS IMMINENT. I have done it and do it. There is SUPPORT for you. JOIN the group of SOLDIERS willing to FIGHT REGARDLESS of their FEAR and emotional experience in the MOMENT and YOU CAN'T LOSE. I implore you to TRY AGAIN. TRY WITH ME. Don't choose apathy. I almost did. DO NOT. I VOWED to help and encourage you to make that POWERFUL CHOICE TO FIGHT as long as there is BREATH IN YOUR BODY... "AS LONG AS THERE IS BREATH IN MY BODY, I WILL FIGHT THIS." How about you? How about those after you?

Recommended Resources

IOCDF – International Obsessive Compulsive Disorder Foundation - www.iocdf.org

Center Pointe Hospital – 4801 Weldon Springs Parkway, St. Charles, MO 63304, 1-800-345-5407

NAMI – National Alliance On Mental Illness, 1-800-950-6264

Show Me OCD Support Groups – led by Gregory Sansone – www.GregorySansone.com, gregorysansone@hotmail.com, showmeocd.com, 636-236-2267

St. Louis OCD Support Group – www.stlocd.org

Personal OCD Recovery Coaching: - Gregory Sansone www.GregorySansone.com, gregorysansone@hotmail.com, 636-236-2267

Speaking Engagements/Seminars – Gregory Sansone www.GregorySansone.com, gregorysansone@hotmail.com, 636-236-2267

Recommended Readings

Tormenting Thoughts & Secret Rituals – Ian Osborn, M.D.

Managing Obsessive Compulsive Disorder: A Sufferer's Question and Answer Guide – Mark L. Berger Ph.D. with commentary by Steven Phillipson, Ph.D.

Don't Panic: Taking Control of Anxiety Attacks – R. Reid Wilson, Ph.D.

Finding X: One Family's Solution to Obsessive Compulsive Disorder – Joni & Ray St. John

Just Checking – Emily Colas

Rewind, Replay, Repeat – Jeff Bell

White Bears & Other Unwanted Thoughts – Daniel M. Wegner

Tao Te Ching – Stephen Mitchell

Karate: The Art of Empty Self – Terrence Webster-Doyle

Taming Your Gremlin: A Guide to Enjoying Yourself – Richard D. Carson

Tiger Heart, Tiger Mind: How To Empower Your Dream – Ron Rubin & Stuart Avery Gold

The Go-Giver – Bob Burg John David Mann

Stillness Speaks – Eckhart Tolle

The Power of Now – Eckhart Tolle

Practicing the Power of Now – Eckhart Tolle

The Little Book of Happiness – Patrick Whiteside

Reflections on the Art of Living: A Joseph Campbell Companion – selected and edited by Diane K. Osbon

Wowisms: Words of Wisdom for Dreamers & Doers – Ron Rubin & Stuart Avery Gold

Get Out of Your Mind & Into Your Life: The New Acceptance & Commitment Therapy – Stephen C. Hayes, Ph.D. with Spencer Smith

OCD Treatment Through Story Telling: A Strategy for Successful Therapy – Allen H. Weg

The Imp of the Mind – Lee Baer, Ph.D.

The Ray of Hope: A Teenager's Guide Against Obsessive Compulsive Disorder – Ray St. John

The Thought That Counts: A 1ˢᵗ Hand Account of (1) Teenagers Experience with OCD – Jared Douglas Kant with Martin Franklin, Ph.D.

Man, Interrupted – James Bailey

Buddhism Plain & Simple – Steve Hagen

Constructive Living – David K. Reynolds

The Richest Man In Babylon – George S. Clason

What Should I Do With My Life? – Po Bronson

Made in the USA
San Bernardino, CA
31 October 2015